# $\mathcal{B}$LUE
## PERIOD
### IN
## SEATTLE

# Blue Period in Seattle

## Period
## in
## Seattle

SELECTED POEMS
(1991-2011)

## JOHN W. GORSKI

iUniverse, Inc.
Bloomington

**Blue Period in Seattle**
**Selected Poems (1991-2011)**

*iUniverse books may be ordered through booksellers or by contacting:*

*iUniverse*
*1663 Liberty Drive*
*Bloomington, IN 47403*
*www.iuniverse.com*
*1-800-Authors (1-800-288-4677)*

*ISBN: 978-1-4620-5416-9 (sc)*
*ISBN: 978-1-4620-5417-6 (ebk)*

*Printed in the United States of America*

*iUniverse rev. date: 09/27/2011*

# Contents

## Blue Period in Seattle ........................................ 57

## About The Author ................................................ 85

# The Man with the Green Face

# The Artist Young and Old
## (After Edvard Munch)

His youthful face —
an April moon
on a Berlin evening —
peered through the haze
of his cigarette.
Something was locked in his eyes
from those deep, blue shadows —
some distant portent
waiting for him in Norway.

His eyes sunken,
he wandered through his rooms,
alone with insomnia.
Bent over with age,
he thought of Europe
descending into war.

*John W. Gorski*

All afternoon, he had sat
with his back to the cold window
where the crisp snow of Skyloven
hung on gray, leafless bones.
White and gray had collected
all those years in his hair,
as he felt the fire leaving his blood.

He roamed on between
clock and bed — his painting
of a nude, corpse-like woman
leering through the dark,
as the journey of his flesh through time
approached her pallor.

## The Dance of Life
## (After Edvard Munch)

The warm moon spills
a gold path like a pillar
fallen across the waters.

Her face rising celestial
from a white-flowered dress,
she greets the summer
evening in Norway.
Passionate couples whirl by
in this party
on the meadow above the bay.

A sober-frocked minister dances
with the young woman
as her long gown winds around
him in an amorous fever.
She moves back and forth —
burning now in a red dress —
her auburn hair spreading to his heart.

*John W. Gorski*

Later, she stands aside —
clad in black and older,
her countenance ashen —
and watches her scarlet younger self
while the other couples continue
to spin by in wild embraces
and devouring masks
like the man with a green face.

# Paris 1918

In cooling white linen,
Apollinaire lay assassinated
by the Spanish flu,
immune to the azure
that once shone over Paris.
It was days before the Armistice
but he had returned two years
early from the trenches
and droning aeroplanes.

Memories of Montparnasse
fevered his brain
where talk of art burned
with wine and stirring manifestos
in salons with Picasso and Braque.

He slowly receded
beneath the lamp-lit gaze
of his new wife, thinking of towns
he had walked through, guided
by his youthful muse.
He began to lose himself
in those villages of red
and yellow leaves masked by fog,
where a peasant's song of spurned love
told how autumn had slain summer.

*John W. Gorski*

Now, the black-printed wings
of his poems in *Calligrammes*
fluttered upon the page
and lifted above the cacophony
of the victory crowds.

# Winslow Homer and the Sea

Past fifty, he lived in Maine
at the edge of the white orchestra
of Atlantic surf,
its cymbals and tympani
invading the dark
of his last hour of sleep.
Then he arose with paints
and brush to render
the spray of breakers
against black rocks
and the salmon-pink line
of dawn in the east
under ragged banners
of slate-blue night clouds.

At noon, the captain
and his second in command
began to materialize
upon his canvas.
They studied a sextant
to "read the sun" on the deck
of their vessel that rolled
up and down on the green
body of the ocean.

*John W. Gorski*

He remembered the pearl-gray
weather of the docks,
as he stood before his easel
one morning and saw
the women waiting there again,
day after day, for the fishing boats
with their husbands to return.

A man of few words,
he portrayed the sea
that resounded with the howls
and cries of the sailors
it had taken in.

## Seraphine de Senlis

Up in her room at night,
behind on the rent,
she lifts a song to God
as she paints by
the light of one candle.
An apple tree buzzing with
the insects she talks to
in the countryside around Senlis
fills her canvas.
Flowers whisper in answer
to her speech while she goes
from village to village
to work as a maid and washerwoman.

She hymns when bathing
in the cold springtime river,
and past midnight she can be heard
upstairs with mortar and pestle,
grinding the plants she scavenges
from her walks to distill
the colors for her palette.

*John W. Gorski*

Then Wilhelm Uhde, an art critic,
discovers her work
and, as it begins to sell
she spends like a madwoman:
furnishing a suite of rooms
and buying a wedding dress.
The morning of the ceremony,
missing a groom,
she wanders the streets
in her flowing white gown,
leaving silverware on doorsteps,
until the constable is called.

She is driven away,
the heavenly voices
still talking in her head,
to the asylum in Clermont.
She spends the rest of her days
in its gray-walled Babel,
looking out the window
at a lone tree on top of a hill.

# Lester Young

His tenor saxophone
moaned on the blue outskirts of town,
its legato phrasing
carrying him to New Orleans
and Kansas City
and finally to New York.
Playing with Count Basie
and Billie Holiday,
his solos floated above
the time of the band
like pale, azure-lit clouds.
In his porkpie hat,
he walked the streets of Manhattan
mouthing inscrutable lingo
to his coterie of sidemen.

He held his golden instrument
at an angle like a flute
and slurred his sparse notes
together to alchemize
a sweet tune.
Like a late-night river,
he coolly drifted
on, telling a story
of a lost October sky
alive with constellations
crooning above the noisy city.

*John W. Gorski*

He burned out in a hotel
where friends brought him
cigarettes and wine.
In his last years,
his audience receded
like a tide off Long Island—
his memory riffing through
thoughts of majesty and regret.

# E. D.'s Noonday Poems — Read a Century Later in NYC

The afternoon was growing late
in the gap between the dime-store satin
of the ash-colored drapes
in the tenement room in Brooklyn.

A man there opened a book
to the white noon of the poet's meadow
before her family house
and read in the lengthening shadows.

He heard the bees buzz in her verse
under the blue helium sky at midday
and the divine harmonies
of orioles on their dazzling way.

All the long-ago prism light
of her meadow poetry repeated
through the Ornette Coleman riffs
the traffic played in the streets.

He thought of her later, veiled
in her room, foreign to the communion
she once had with the singing
grass and air beyond her seclusion.

*John W. Gorski*

As his sepia hands turned
the pages exalting the 12 o'clock sun,
the city twilight spilled
like cheap red wine between the curtains.

Closing the book, he listened
to carousing in the street and the el
screeching like a hoot owl to
a stop at ten-minute intervals.

# Season of Insomnia

This morning, a gray ocean sky
in a familiar choral lament
sang over the Seattle hills,
after days of salsa sun played
the fiery brass of its festival
between the dark, cobalt sleep
of the night's cooling intervals.
For weeks, I have heard the leap
of electronic beats rattle
the floor and rumble the ground
until the alley's sounds
pierced my heart in rhythms
that suddenly assassinated
temporary equilibriums.

Only Highway 99,
under its carbon monoxide veil
with its steady engines
like fracturing lullabies,
can offer oblivion.

*John W. Gorski*

I have grown drowsy in my car
parked by the shimmering oblong
of Green Lake where youthful joggers
race by in sleek rainbows of Lycra,
while the past appears again over
my left shoulder like some pale
afternoon of confusing murmurs.
Under the trees, some people
are dancing to tribal drummers
thundering a deep frenzy
that catches the drunken whimsy
of a vagrant's attention,
who laughs in a whiskey-drenched voice
and wails the word "reincarnation."

# Hejira at the Metal Arts Collective (1/9/10)

The midnight heart of the Oud
pulses in the rhythms
Don strums on his guitar.
A crescent moon glints
off the bow of Ashraf's cello,
as his fingers blaze
up and down the strings
under a broken necklace
of red neon lights
that hang from the ceiling
of an electronic cave
with meandering dogs
on a Saturday night.

For the audience
come in from a cold overcast,
they play like a small orchestra,
ringing with the mountains
and faraway
constellations of Morocco.

*John W. Gorski*

A Mediterranean surf
sunlit with morning
rolls on the screen behind them
as their jazz chords wrap around
classical reveries.
The notes they play
grow and mutate,
like the images
the projectionist transmits
of wine-drenched rubies
and blinding diamonds
that shine above a green forest
and close in a nocturne —
of Prussian blue stars.

# Assemblages by Al Slobodin

Junkyard baby doll
scrapes a one-string violin
to the joker card
framed in bric-a-brac,
a pair of dice
reading eleven at her feet.

Matted, synthetic hair,
one eye closed,
the other looking toward
a field of night growing
tubers and strawberries,
and a Greek god
astride a watermelon slice.

Her drone serenades
an anatomical man
reaching out to take
the hand of Venus haloed
by a lemon-yellow moon.

Skull stares out
through a window in the dark;
a skeleton leans
on a bony shovel
in granite shadows.

# Flamenco Sunlight

The jazz station plays flamenco
sunlight through the hemlock and the fir
of a February hillside.
The gray Seattle winter
is waiting to be reborn
into the green breathing
of the leaves and grass that return
with the April sun.
The cars go by on 99
at forty miles per hour,
detached from the sublime
music that forgets
the morning rain that scrolled
across the sky with its regrets.

A Mediterranean scene
rolls an aqua sea through the mind
grown warm and Andalusian.
The midafternoon coastline
rings with gypsy cafés
of clicking castanets
and strumming strings amid a craze
of black stamping feet.
But these moments leave in exile,
backward into the cold air
of the bitter, asphalt miles
that brought them here,
to pale like apparitions
in the brooding, charcoal atmosphere.

There is only this moment
and the next and the next —
notes plucked from a Spanish guitar
to sing of the invisible stars.

# Rainy Day Haiku

Magnesium voices read verse
to refugees from rainy streets
within walls the color
of Roquefort cheese.

# Relative
# Damnation

# Charmed Estuary

Through my twenties,
the Chesapeake would reach
out its tidewater arms
in the waking dark before day,
the sunlight upon it
infused with the memory
of my sister's blonde hair.

Almost seventeen, I entered
a city of hills bordered
by the serpent's coil
of the Ohio River.
With my family, I rode through
the sallow-faced Bavarian streets
past the weathered brick
of Catholic churches
spiring the Lucite gray
of overcast, Midwestern skies.

*John W. Gorski*

One summer five years later,
I found myself
in Mt. Airy forest
wrapped in a murky, charcoal night.
A hound was tracking me
with hallucinogen breath,
strobe eyes, and the snarl
of a thousand out of tune violins.
I waited until his howl
stopped ringing in my bloodstream
and finally came, fractured,
to a white pastel sun
filling an upstairs room
in my parents' house.

I would never return
to the laughter under the green
oaks along the shores
of that gull-voiced estuary,
after my sister left us.

# Street Prophet

Sunday in the holding cells.
*Dark Side of the Moon* drifted a stream
of radio static down the row.
He held his right hand — a soot-stained swan —
over his eyes against
the interrogation of the light bulb.

The cops just saw a young crazy
jabbering signs and revelations.
They didn't understand
the scriptures in his head
voicing a dark prophecy
and a beacon for the saved
to follow to a safe zone
near the Equator
in the coming nuclear holocaust.
The next day, they called
a court-appointed shrink
who determined he reached this precipice
whenever he went off lithium.

*John W. Gorski*

Like a good friend, I visited him
at Cincinnati General the next week.
His latest episode tamed,
he paced the fluorescent limbo
of the psych ward,
squinting his glass-bead eyes.
He told about his mother
hallucinating on her deathbed
when he was nine, and his sister
and him saying the rosary
during the Cuban Missile Crisis.

In a few months, I left the Bavarian
street names climbing the hills
of his hometown
and his voice faded
in the gray, pierced by seabird cries
over Elliot Bay.

# Virgil's Farewell to the Pilgrim

"You have come with the ragged
pulse of a dove;
the hope is small
in your sad Florentine voice.
Now from the continent of the Ganges,
I give you an angel of God.
Beautiful world — all three
hundred and sixty degrees
and the planets voyaging out
into the unknown continuum."

"Beautiful world," roars
a lion in the hills
of a stained-glass forest on fire.
"You must rise and wander through
these corridors of flaming trees
on your way to Paradise.
Forget the lash
that torments your flesh;
you must pursue the quest of your faith
on wings of ash."

"Geryon has come from the eighth circle
to point you toward salvation.
The spirits of Limbo still
echoing in my head, I leave for home.
The burning cadenza of your journey
is at hand and then you will
enter in an eye blink,
the blinding white that takes all in."

## Relative Damnation — Dante Reports from Cincinnati (1975)

From native tribes, a sepia-green spiral
of the Ohio was taken by whites who built
a town there named after a Roman general.
It prospered with riverboat commerce
until the locomotive mostly bypassed
the city thus leaving it for the worse.
Meanwhile, Germans with alien tongues and ways
poured in, appalling local society
with their habit of drinking beer on Sunday.

Now, I arrive in the coal fires
of a July twilight more than a century
later when the hills of oak and maple perspire.
Young people try to stay cool playing Foosball
in tank tops and shorts in dank basements
where all night they chug six-packs of Hudepohl.
Real estate salesmen in polyester flares
and plaid jackets seek refuge in bars
from the withered lawns and damp laundry air.

*John W. Gorski*

In discos, those imprisoned in big-collar shirts
*Get Up and Boogie* to music that implies:
"You vill boogie und you vill like it."
Televisions blare through windows of domiciles
that Pete Rose just stole second and replay
over and over his amphetamine hustle.
Rats lie DOA from tainted five-way chili
they feasted on in alleys behind restaurants
serving up that local delicacy.

At dawn, the slap of the *Enquirer*
sounds on the driveway, its invective of ink
prepared to smudge the mind of the reader.
Like a Republican candidate, it rants
about the IRS and communists
who want to put fluoride in the water supply.
But it still hasn't predicted the worst fear
of its nineteen fifty-five mind set:
that of Jerry Springer becoming the next mayor.

# A Rat Approaches Dante's Purgatory (circa 1976)

The news chopper descends
from a cardboard gray Ohio sky
to a knot of groundlings
standing around a parking slot
on Court Street.
There a rat lies dead,
sideswiped by one of Cincinnati's finest.

"Maybe he didn't pay the meter,"
a guy from Northside jokes. "Carses, where
am I going to park my Camaro," a teenage girl
from Western Hills rants. "Appalling,"
an Indian Hill matron huffs.
"Are there no rat mortuaries?" she continues.
"It couldn't have been much fun,"
the reporter intones in his double-knit
polyester suit, "this gutter life
scrambling past platform heels and disco boots."
"Yeah, no Foosball or bleacher seats
at Riverfront Stadium, no keggers,"
a young man says. "No rollercoaster
rides at Kings Island or
dancing at the Black Stallion,
no Laverne and Shirley," a young woman adds.
"Yeah," they all Greek-chorus.

*John W. Gorski*

Meanwhile, the rat looks down
at the overcast pallor of his tiny form
and sees himself skittering across
the shards of a broken mirror
in the hulk of an abandoned building
in Over-the-Rhine.
Suddenly, he stops at the cliff-edge
of a coastal woods
with psychotic lions and mutant wolves,
where Beatrice appears in saffron robes
of sunrise over a blue lullaby
of Lake Erie.

# A Bullet from Stones River

With a child's hand, I held
the century-old bullet
my great-grandmother found
buried in her garden in Tennessee:
an errant death message sent
when the battle of Stones River
spilled into Murfreesboro.

Under the pallor of morning sky
the day after the fighting ended,
two journalists lounged
against a wagon's wheels
in a clearing amid cedars,
where wren harmonies woke
the air in counterpoint
to the rifle fire
still crackling in their heads.

*John W. Gorski*

They talked about the last three days —
the eve of the battle with its jests
and laughter around winter campfires
and a banjo frailing "Pretty Peggy-O";
the next morning when columns
of blue and gray armies
turned to packs of demons
lunging with bayonets;
the afternoon of perishing soldiers
with the graveyard in their eyes,
their flesh to become earth
as they lay in the field
where transparencies of men
rose above their bodies
that crows embroidered
in an eternity of icy rain.

The journalists rode
the jerk and rattle
of country roads all night to Lebanon
to find this cloud-roofed sanctuary
where they could close their eyes.

# Noonday Vignettes

I.

Women of an occult society
appear through a lens of sleep
in neck-to-toe Victorian dresses
with sober-suited men
standing or lounging on a grassy hillside
embraced by sycamores.
The minister intones
wedding vows from a secret book,
while the bride in body-length white
holds the wooden hand
of the twenty-foot oak-carved groom,
whose face rises primeval
in the blinding sun for hours
until the sky turns
to red wine "spill'd on lips
and bosoms by touching glasses"
at the twilight feast.

*John W. Gorski*

II.


Sun-filled voices
of ten-year-old girls dapple
the noon hour oxygen
of the public square
at a May Day celebration.
Braids of their black hair dance
when they whirl and chant
anthems to the *Great Leader*
whose face looms along highways
and covers sides of buildings.
The bright air of festivities
is divided by telephone wires
that carry the chatter of his agents
and rivers of Peking dialect,
informing "against my brother and sister"
whose allegiance is questioned
in police stations.


*Quoted phrases are from the poems of Walt Whitman.

# Two Yellow Butterflies

alit on father's black coat,
as he drove the wagon
into an ocean of gold light
on a "boisterous afternoon"
of his children's laughter
spilling from the jostling shadows
of passing sycamores.
When one butterfly found itself
upon the horse-trampled road,
Emily grew pensive,
thinking of her mother's admonition
not to "take cold" in the halcyon
façade of April weather.
Suddenly, she knew
the arpeggios of laughter
were only day-lit moments
that would drown in the vast sea
of dark awaiting everyone.

*John W. Gorski*

She recalled later how, as
a child in church, the clergyman
invited "all those who loved
the Lord Jesus Christ to remain" —
and the pleasure of thus
being allowed to leave.
In her last years, she again
glimpsed his faceless sire
abstracted to a distance,
as she witnessed
the typhoid countenance
of her eight-year-old nephew
and the blond rays
of his hair on a sickbed.

*All phrases in quotes are from letters of Emily Dickinson
and her family.

# Transcript in Illness
## (Susan Gilbert Writes to a Friend)

"Earthly pleasures are so mutable"
I see, as the cold Atlantic tide
advances under a winding sheet
of Marblehead gray
toward this night in Amherst.
I am weak from my "confinement
to bed so long," drifting
in the crimson lamplight
of fever as I sense
a surf rolling in
beneath the windows of this house.

I remember walking downhill
with "our gentlemen"
after a lecture last year
"under the escort" of summer stars.
Last night when I looked out,
the constellations danced
their skeletons in the blue-black sky.

*John W. Gorski*

The idea of marriage
"when Austen returns" from Chicago
in the withering months
of leaves withdrawing their palms
"seems absurd enough."
He in a raven-dark suit
and I in wraith white
will lead a procession
to announce our becoming
a link between the flesh
that has been and will be.

But first I must regain my strength
and the rose-pink immanence
of the morning horizon.

*All quoted phrases are from the letters of Susan Gilbert,
the sister-in-law of Emily Dickinson.

# Post-War Vignettes

Fires spew from brick towers
in the valley of Hades, Nevada,
circa 1947.
A town of worker's
barracks and shacks
decay around a copper smelter,
its men imprisoned
in a clockwork twilight
around furnaces at the earthen
depression of arid mountainsides
stained with ash.

Five young men lean against
the soot-dimmed windows
of the town's general store —
Chicago boys out west
in dungarees, laced-up boots,
and cocksure grins —
strangers to diseased lungs.
In their eyes, a cobalt mirage
of the Pacific gleams
at the end of Route 66.

*John W. Gorski*

On an ocean-clouded corner
in San Francisco in 1958,
one of the five—who was blinded at work—
wears a beret and wheezes
"My Funny Valentine"
on a pawnshop accordion.
A young woman drops some coins
in the case by his white cane
in a shutter-click of time and place,
lost in a spiraling cosmos,
inscribing infinite dark.

## Cuckoo in the Wrong Habitat—North Seattle (1990s)

"Psych, Cuckoo" the twelve-year-old girl
upstairs chirped, as he closed
the door to laughing street eyes
after coming home from work.
A strange bird: He lived solitary
in the thickets of imagination,
in the dusty willow branches
of squandered time.

His brain began to seethe
with the staccato aria
of a yellow-billed call that knew
the lament of an approaching storm
and the black specks on the face
of the sun overhead.
It wound around his thoughts
like the playing children's voices,
the engines turning over,
stereos throbbing
in the boom-box alley
next to his window.
Outside his door, two acolytes
of Beavis and Butthead listened
to his telephone conversation
after getting bored one day
with skateboarding down the hall.

*John W. Gorski*

He should have known better
than to live here among
these Desert Storm-clad denizens
whose TVs lit up
with professional wrestling,
whose parents turned the dial
to Red, White, and Blue country music,
whose sons swaggered like Kid Rock;
should have known they would realize
from hearing him use "big words"
that he had a library card—
but the rent was cheap.
So, he could only wait
until his wallet fattened
and then fly south with a prescription
for a tricyclic in his beak.

# Thought Weary

Umbrella of soft, rainy clouds
above Third Avenue
as the clock strikes twelve times
this August Saturday
of hypnotized minds.
All the drunken vagabonds
wear the clothes of young men
as they weave down the concrete
with a misty shoreline
in their sleepy, seasick eyes —
looking ready to drown
in the gray of Puget Sound.

But ain't it great
to be waiting for the #358
within an afternoon
of anonymous fate.

*John W. Gorski*

The late twentieth century
monoliths spear the sky
over the asphalt static
of cigarette voices
and ranting lunatics.
On the bus, I watch overcast
highway scenes through the hole
in another rider's earlobe,
as the hour's silent toll
gets lost in speeding engines,
reeling old memories
into new cacophonies.

But ain't it great
to be riding on the #358
into an afternoon
of anonymous fate.

# Momentary Speck

Woke up too late today —
now it's afternoon
and my mind is humming
a skeleton's tune.
I'm creaking back and forth
round in circles,
waiting for the bus to
downtown Seattle.
Soon, Green Lake flickers through
the drifting fir trees,
as the passengers talk
in Jabberwocky.

Under the cold, blue robe
of this December sky,
I'm a momentary speck
where the icy majesty
of sunlight and street intersect.

*John W. Gorski*

Sea gulls call above
the thousands of eyes,
roaming concrete, lost to
their white, arcing cries.
Estranged from the land
surrounding this town,
crowds sip coffee and spin
their words round and round.
So, I just keep walking
amid alcohol
and caffeine-buzzed voices,
looking for my soul.

Under the cold, blue robe
of this December sky,
I'm a momentary speck
where the icy majesty
of sunlight and street intersect.

# Mumblestiltskin

A mild-mannered, ogre dwarf
with a muffled voice,
he dances around the fire
wherever he roams
in castoff styles from Goodwill,
a size too big.

Silent and anxiety-riddled
on the bus,
he weaves golden phrases —
or so he thinks —
from the scraps
of passengers' conversation
on the wheel humming in his mind.

People must ask him
to repeat himself sometimes
when his words sound
from the rat cellar
of his vocal cords,
so he chooses not to speak.

*John W. Gorski*

At night he falls
into a forest of sleep
where the animals greet each other
with cordial salutations.
But soon the tranquil woods morph
into a metropolis
of humans whose glancing remarks
tear him in two,
and then he wakes speechless
from the jerking video
of his medicated slumber.

# The 4 Loko Bus

Lately, the 4 Loko bus
has sobered up;
this afternoon, you almost expect
a game of Scrabble to break out
as we ride past Lake Union
under serge gray clouds
into downtown Seattle.

It's so different now
from the Christmas season
last month when one day a man
claimed the dachshund he brought
aboard was bipolar.
"Yeah, so is my parakeet,"
a woman next to him
chimed in. "He's been talking garbage
lately; that's why I left
him at home today."
Then another man got on
with a weathered Freddy Fender
album and said "I bought this
for my girlfriend in Yakima.
Johnny Mathis, Gonzaga University — do you
feel the Holy Spirit?"

So I began
climbing the five blocks of hills
to catch the NPR bus,
which most days resembled
the rare books room of a library
compared to the Greyhound Bus station
of the route I eschewed.

But today, the first route returns
to its caffeinated, alcohol buzz
as a middle-aged guy with long, gray hair
asserts through broken teeth:
"I smoked four packs and drank
a gallon of beer everyday
for ninety-two years."
"Boy, you must have really had
a problem," a guy across from him says.
"No," he replied, "I was just
trying to keep up with my dog."

# Blue Period
# in Seattle

## Autumn Fugue

Unearthly alabaster temple
of her face turned upward —
she lay in a blue satin dress —
blonde hair pulled back from her brow,
eyes closed to the ceiling,
while the living in black
revolved around her body.

Clouds had vanished
above the graphite streets
as we set forth
in the halogen-lit procession,
carrying the speechless girl
up the yellow and ocher-thronged
hills of Cincinnati
under the blind gaze
of an October sun
that burned us to the marrow
with the knowledge
of her departure.

*John W. Gorski*

In the ritual landscape
of green lawns and marble,
two ministers offered
biblical passages and prayers
at the invisible altar
of the unknown,
their words floating away
into the nothingness
of a balmy afternoon.

And then we drove back
to the daily charade,
to drown every evening
in the deepest valley
of an ocean,
and to wake on a shore of morning light
charged with her absence.

# The Chesapeake's Waters

I'll never get back
to the choir of indecipherable words
carried on sea breezes
from the inlets of the Chesapeake
when I was a child in Maryland.
In the summer's humidity,
they gleamed like sunlight
in the waves of my sister's blonde hair
and faded in a blue Polaroid haze.

Soon twilight filled
the beginning of my teens
with the vermilion harmonies
of the Drifters singing
"This Magic Moment,"
a rhapsody of ecstatic sentences
repeating from convertibles sailing
down Ritchie Highway from Baltimore.

*John W. Gorski*

But we moved away,
and my sister left forever,
stranding us under the azure
himmel of Cincinnati
where I got lost
in the hiss of German syllables.
Riding the haunted green
night hills above the river,
I saw my sister, a wraith
watching the Ohio winding west.

Later, I boarded
the raga juggernaut
of the Stones' "Paint It Black,"
seeking an Eden where my brain
caught fire with hallucinogens
and I descended to solitude
as the evening sun darkened
to a blot of India ink.

# Gray Sun in Late Winter

A gray sun winks
in the Puget Sound sky
I ride under on the bus
this March afternoon
on Fourth Avenue South.

A woman in a burgundy cap
two rows ahead of me
glances out the window,
taking me back to 1977
and another woman
six years older than me.
I remember how she once
put on an oversized beret
of the same color
and called it her "go to hell hat."

And now everything
from that year comes back:
the day she told me
about the radio station
she heard playing music
in the fillings of her teeth
and wondered if I could hear it too;
the evenings she spoke
of the "fugue states"
she phased into
on the medicine she used

*John W. Gorski*

to control her epilepsy;
her eyes blinking
through nicotine veils of smoke
as her cats meowed
around the living room;
the times she read
the light and shadow
of her nervous breakdown poems
from the penciled longhand
of green notebook pages;
the October afternoon
I mouthed the fading rosebuds
of her nipples,
and the next weekend when
she taught me the undulations
of her sallow body—
taking me into a trembling
heaven of electricity
I hadn't known before.

And now I think
of the gulf of years
widening between us
and the sentence I serve
for outliving her
and not seeing the dark horizon
gathering in her last phone call.

# Sonnet in February

I woke from a rainy, charcoal street
into a dry room of muted yellow
where cold gave way to the temperate heat
of a conversation deep as marrow.

A gazelle woman sat across the room
on a futon by a sea of lamplight;
my vision was captured by the bloom
of her opaline face — a knowing light.

She spoke of premonitions and past lives
and the concept of synchronicity
and how the departed had grown more wise
living in their bodiless mystery.

Her eyes pierced transient winter gray
like the dawning light of a cloudless day.

# Arctic Willow

Glacier light in her brown eyes
surveys a page of my verse,
suggesting phrases to be condensed,
minimalist sleights of hand.
The arctic willow watches
from a cold shelf in my mind,
murmuring a continuum;
plants grow in meticulous
pottery in the pallid
winter light of her windows.

Suddenly, she laughs—
a songbird's trills
between the convent-white
walls of her apartment.
She smiles—her face opening
like an avalanche lily,
as she tells me of
Sufi visions and ghosts
of her Catholic past.
Our eyes meet—umber and azure—
only to find scattered
flickers of harmony.

Hours of talk are gone
by late afternoon.
We hug and she sends me out
into the gray noise
of Seattle streets
to catch the fluorescent transit
with my icy companion
of snow-petal stalks
to an address
above the timberline.

# April Rain — North Seattle

The afternoon sky broods
in gray ceilings of nostalgia
as my eye follows
the damp asphalt of a street
climbing the green horizon
of hemlock and cedar.

The wind breathes white-blossomed trees,
their scent making me wonder
how many days I've seen like this —
looking through the silks
of rain layering this neighborhood.

A wheel of gulls
turns in the distance
and scatters,
only to reassemble
in a circle of memory.

Miles away a boat
hoots out on the waters
of an invisible past.

# Blue Period in Seattle

August morning sifts the silent
speech of clouds over
Third Avenue until
the Metro radio crackles
with a century-old voice.
"It's eleven a.m. in the eternal city,"
a man says in a Catalan tongue.

In a seat across from me,
a passenger's newspaper
is turning the ashen blue of Picasso's
canvases in 1903 Barcelona,
the wraith sister of Seattle.
As I listen to their shallow breathing,
the streets fill up with
the colors of his paint box
and the figures he portrayed.

The old guitarist plays
in an alley between condominiums,
his ragged lament
shattered by the seismic beat
of a passing car stereo.
Mediterranean gulls wheel
above the slow tarantella
of reeling drunks
on the Belltown sidewalks.

*John W. Gorski*

A man and woman and their small boy
walk in the waterfront park
a hundred years later
by the cold, metallic waters
of Puget Sound
in the same poverty.

# Childhood Sky

When I was four in Delaware,
I followed my father and sister
down the wind-filled blocks of row houses
to an empty lot
where the strings of kites
unraveled in the hands
of older children.
I watched the shuddering ascent
in the March azure
and felt the inverse
of the claustrophobic dark
of covered bridges we drove
through over the Brandywine river
outside of Wilmington.

*John W. Gorski*

At twenty, I was lying on
my bed in Cincinnati
beneath Wyeth's *Christina's World*,
listening to a Beatles album.
I was hearing the nuances
of bass and rhythm guitar
more clearly than ever before,
after smoking hash for the first time.
I closed my eyes and once again
the children flew their kites
in the springtime blue
that had turned warmer
and then I was in a swing
lifting toward those heights
and down and up again.

In a North Seattle office,
a calm morning voice questions
that mid-Atlantic sky,
now a corroded whisper
amid the Babel of laughter and car horns
intersecting the cloudy streets.

# Ballad of a Five-Year-Old Sheriff

Sheriff with a runny nose —
smallest five-year-old
in all of the neighborhood —
under a cowboy hat and holding
a cap gun, he sure looked good.

He was the law thereabouts,
roaming the frontier
of Harundale, Maryland,
looking for bad guys shorter than him
on that suburban Rio Grande.

Wearing a polo shirt
in that black and white photograph,
he looked like a good excuse
for an adult belly laugh.

Fearsome in his saddle shoes
and seersucker shorts — or so his parents said —
he searched for other kids who would
agree to fall down and play dead.

But all the phony gunfire
suddenly stopped
when the ice cream truck played
its recorded bells or his mom
called him in for Kool-Aid.

*John W. Gorski*

This went on till autumn cold
drove him inside to
play Space Commander to all
of the milk and cookie aliens
he could find to hold in his thrall.

# My Paternal Grandfather

"*Gott in die Himmel*," he grumbled
down a street in Queens
still damp with night rain,
while a block away
the 6:45 a.m. el
sailed like a Chagall violinist
into the dingy, watercolor light
above the rooftops.
He had lingered
too long over butterhorns
and coffee, reminiscing with his wife
about his immigrant father's
stories of the Baltic Sea.

Now he paced the train platform
in a 1940's anxiety, his arteries
hardening, as he looked west
to Brooklyn and the East River
where he operated bridges
for the City of New York.

*John W. Gorski*

I only know him —
my paternal grandfather —
through old black and white
photographs and my own worries
about being late.
One cold April day
in 1951, he walked
out to mail a letter
in his shirtsleeves
and inhaled a dark herald
of the pneumonia
that stopped his breath.

## Vacations in Tennessee

In the blueberry dark
alive with lightnin' bugs
and the Tennessee cadences
of my grandparents' speech,
we sat on the front porch
to cool off from a July day
in Murfreesboro.
My grandfather carved
a backwoods preacher from cherry wood,
while my grandmother rambled on
about "Aint" Minnie
and the other relatives
in Mackenzie who helped
raise her after her mother died.

Every summer, my family spent
two weeks in this world of
warm, languishing accents and rolling hills
so different from our home
in the suburbs of Baltimore.
Me and my sister and brother
played catch and ran around
in the maple shade
of my grandparents' backyard.
By afternoon, we were
sampling the cold drinks
from the refrigerator:

*John W. Gorski*

all the "Ara Cee" cola,
Nehi orange, and Dr. Pepper
we were allowed per day.
Some evenings, we visited
the air conditioned-paradise
of my great-aunts' homes,
where they offered us
clove-flavored chewing gum.

After my grandfather died,
my grandmother came to live
with us for a while in Ohio.
From time to time,
she got letters from Murfreesboro
telling of the death
of another of her woman friends,
and she cried as she recalled
their voices fading out
like the whisper of poplar trees.

# Smoky Room of Jazz

Overcast has brooded in my eyes
all week, down the winter skyway
I drive under this afternoon
on the road skirting Elliot Bay.
Soon I reach my destination
and enter Crysta's room
of smoky jazz, where rumination
sounds from a clarinet.
It plays out the drunken regret
in the heart of all those clubs
of Greenwich Village in the '50s,
as a film rolls in my memory
of black and white scenes of Manhattan
streets beneath a gray, celluloid sun.

Somewhere in my cloudy mind I hear
a saxophone reaching
a plangent note intermittently,
like a boat horn miles out at sea.

*John W. Gorski*

As I leave Crysta's, she looks like
a young woman again at the door
and then I walk through Belltown rain
to the cocoon of my parked car.
I watch gnarled tree branches along
the sidewalk gather me
into an old age of dimming song,
forgetting my reason.
Now as the cold of the season
burns on the skeleton mask
of my skin, I look through the windshield
at drifting people and chrome car wheels
riding by the glowering street lights
turning day to a theatre of night.

## Apparitions of a Winter Night

I get off the bus
at Sixty-fourth and Linden
because the dark organ chords
of alcohol laughter
are playing out of tune
in a chaos that drowns sound waves.

It is twilight
after hours of rain;
a cloud like a tattered, purple gown
from a wedding reception
fifty years ago blows northward.
The groom carries his top hat
filled with missing conversations,
and the maid of honor
takes home the bouquet,
her pre-Raphaelite face
a lunar masque
advancing out of the night.

*John W. Gorski*

Yellow and red neon
from the Aurora Avenue
business district undulates
on the waters of Green Lake.
A bicyclist whirs past
like a shadow
of my twelve-year-old self,
as cold portals of azure
shine through the indigo
fabric of the heavens.
I walk home by
the recently installed
antique lamps that draw
pen and ink bare branches
on a reflection of my face
passing a shop window.

# Liquid Reflection

Down the dampening asphalt
thoroughfares of North Seattle
I have driven,
*The Windows of the World*
playing on a loop in my head.

Alone in my car
parked at Green Lake,
I'm caught in the continuum
of looking back.

The side mirrors,
like rainy eyes, fill
with the latticework
of bare branches
amid blackening hemlock
and the halogen stares of vehicles
rolling down the road behind me.
As dark comes on,
lights from the eastern shore
of the lake bleed
onto its cold surface.

When I leave,
a singer on the radio
becomes a ventriloquist
for the absent moon.

# About The Author

John Gorski has a B.A. in English Literature from the University of Cincinnati. He has studied poetry writing at the University of Washington Extension and the Richard Hugo House in Seattle. He grew up primarily in Maryland and Ohio and has lived in Seattle since 1976.